•Fun with English•

Word Origins

George Beal
Illustrated by Peter Stevenson

KINGfISHER

General editor: John Grisewood
Editor: Nicola Barber
Illustrations: Peter Stevenson
　　　　　　(Kathy Jakeman Illustration)
Design: Robert Wheeler Associates

KINGFISHER
Kingfisher Publications Plc
New Penderel House, 283–288 High Holborn,
London WC1V 7HZ

This edition published by Kingfisher Publications Plc 2000
10 9 8 7 6 5 4 3 2 1
1(TR)/0100/EDK/(MA)/135EDI

The material in this edition was previously published
by Kingfisher Publications Plc in the *Wordmaster* series
(1993) and in the *Kingfisher Book of Words* (1991)

A CIP catalogue record for this book is available from
the British Library

ISBN 0 7534 0457 5

Printed in Spain

English has developed into the modern language that we speak and write through a long history of influences since the early Anglo-Saxon (Old English) form. The Normans spoke a type of French which became intermixed with Anglo-Saxon, but even before that the Romans had introduced Latin to England. In the centuries that followed, English adopted words from all over the world, and new ones are always coming into use. In recent years *apartheid* (from Afrikaans), *glasnost* and *perestroika* (from Russian) have come into the English language, and this process goes on continuously. The following list gives the history of some interesting English words.

aardvark This name was given to the animal by the Dutch settlers in South Africa. It means 'earth-pig', although an aardvark is actually a kind of anteater.

academy Originally a Greek word from the name of the Greek legendary hero Academus. A gymnasium (school) in the outskirts of Athens was named after him, and was later used to describe other places of learning.

adder is an Old English word *naedre*, meaning 'snake'. The modern German word is *natter*. The word in English lost its 'n' because, when referring to 'a nadder' (as the word once was), the 'n' was mistakenly moved to make the expression 'an adder'.

admiral is of Arabic origin and comes from the word *amir*, meaning 'prince' or 'leader', first used to describe chieftains on land and sea. The letter 'd' crept in because of the similarity to the word 'admire'.

aftermath is made up of 'after' and 'math', the second word being an old English form of 'mowing'. This is because the word 'aftermath' originally referred to a second crop of grass.

agnostic This is quite a new word, invented in 1869 by T.H. Huxley, the scientist. 'Gnostics' were an early Christian sect claiming mystic knowledge, and the 'a' in front denotes 'without such knowledge'.

alcohol is from the Arabic, and means 'fine black powder'. 'Kohl' is still used as eye make-up by many women. Later the word was applied to fine distilled liquids, and finally was used for a spirit of wine.

3

alligator comes from the Latin word *lacertus*. The name came to English through Spanish. The Spanish for alligator is *lagarto*, and the Spanish word for 'the' is *el*. When *el lagarto* was heard by English speakers, it sounded like the one word 'alligator'.

ambush comes from an Old French word meaning 'to hide in the bushes', and is taken from an even earlier Roman word meaning 'to put into a wood'. So it has come to mean 'to take someone by surprise'.

anaconda is a word which comes from Sri Lanka, and means 'lightning stem'. It originally described a whip-snake, but was used by mistake to describe a much larger South American boa.

answer is an Anglo-Saxon word, the second half coming from the same root as 'swear'. It once meant to swear a solemn oath in reply to a charge. The first part 'an' means 'against', so the whole word meant 'to swear against'.

apostrophe comes from the Greek, meaning 'turned away', and was once used to mean 'turning aside to address someone'. It was later applied to the punctuation mark meaning something omitted or 'turned away'.

apricot was once spelled 'apricock', and came into English through French, Portuguese and Arabic from Latin. The last half of the word comes from Latin *praecox* 'early-ripe', a word also related to 'precocious'.

archipelago originally meant 'Aegean Sea'. This sea has many islands, and so the word came to mean a number of islands. The word is Greek, formed from *archi* 'main, principal' and *pelagos* 'sea'.

armadillo is a Spanish word meaning 'armed man' or 'little armoured one', which is apt for an animal whose body is almost entirely encased in a kind of protective armour.

atlas comes from the name of the Titan in Greek mythology who was condemned by the gods to hold up the sky. His name was given to mountains in North Africa and to the Atlantic Ocean. In the 16th century the figure of Atlas often appeared in the front of books of maps. Other similar books came to be called 'atlases'.

attorney comes from the French, and is based on the word 'turn'. It applies to someone to whom people turn for help, especially in legal matters.

about the 16th century, this became a lute-like instrument with the name 'bandore' which became mispronounced as 'banjo'. Another explanation is that 'banjo' derives from the word *mbanza*, a similar instrument from North Africa.

barber comes from the Latin *barba* 'beard', because in early times a barber's work was largely concerned with trimming and cutting beards.

bayonet comes from the town of Bayonne in France, which is where these weapons were originally made. The 'et' ending means something small, as in cigarette 'a small cigar'.

beg comes from the word 'beggar', and not the other way about. The word 'beggar' comes from the Old French *bégard*, a 13th-century begging monk which, in turn, is taken from Lambert le Begue the founder of the Christian sisterhood called the Beguines.

biscuit came to English from French, but the word originates in the Medieval Latin *bis coctus* 'twice baked'.

badminton is from a place-name. It was named after the country house of the Duke of Beaufort, Badminton House in the county of Avon, England, where the game was first played in the middle of the 19th century.

bald originally meant 'having a white patch' and not just hairless. A common name for an inn in England is the 'Bald Faced Stag'. This phrase meant that the animal had a white patch on its face.

banjo has two possible origins. In Latin and Greek the word *pandura* was the name for a musical instrument sacred to the Greek god, Pan. In Europe, up to

5

blackmail The second part of this word 'mail' comes from Scotland, and means 'payment, tax or tribute'. Blackmail is a 16th-century word for the tribute demanded by rebel chiefs in return for their protection.

Bolshevik is a Russian word which comes from the word *bolshoi*, meaning 'big'. A 'Bolshevik' was a member of the majority socialist party. The others were called 'Mensheviks' (from *menshiy* 'less').

bonfire was, in the 14th century, a 'bone-fire' – an open-air burning of bones. Bone-burning was a common event until the beginning of the 19th century, with bones saved especially for the purpose.

boss is of Dutch origin, but first came into English in the United States. It comes from the word *baas* 'master', which earlier had meant 'uncle'.

boycott is named after a person. He was Captain C.C. Boycott, an Irish landlord, who, in the 1880s, was excluded from the Irish Land League after charging his tenants unreasonable rents.

brandy is a shortened form of 'brandywine'. 'Brand' was a word connected with burning, so brandywine means 'burned wine'. In fact the spirit was not burned, but distilled over a hot fire.

bridegroom The 'groom' in this case is nothing to do with horses. In fact, the original word was 'gome', which meant 'man'. The word 'groom' crept in by mistake.

buccaneer comes from the French *boucanier*, the name for a hunter who dried and stored meat on a wooden frame called a 'boucan'. These people were to be found on the island of San Domingo in the West Indies. Later, the word was applied generally to pirates.

bungalow comes from a Hindi word *bangla* meaning 'belonging to Bengal', where thatched, one-storey houses were found.

bunkum is an American word taken from Buncombe, a county in North Carolina. It was used to mean 'nonsense' after a series of inane speeches by the Congressional representative for Buncombe between 1819 and 1821.

butler comes from the Old French word *bouteillier*, describing a man who put wine into bottles. The Normans brought the word to England as *buteler*.

cabinet comes from the same root as 'cabin', meaning a small room. Such a room was often used for displaying works of art, and the word was later applied to a small case used for the same purpose.

calculate comes from the Latin *calculare* 'to calculate', and from *calculus* 'a pebble'. Small stones were used for counting and calculating. The Latin *calx* meant 'a counter' and 'limestone', and is also the origin of our word 'chalk'.

candle comes from a Latin word introduced into England at the beginning of the seventh century as *candela*, from the word *candere*, meaning 'to shine'.

card comes from the French *carte*, and in turn from Latin *charta*. This originally meant 'a papyrus leaf', and later 'paper'. It was taken from the Greek *chartes*, also meaning 'a papyrus leaf'. Both in English and French, the word 'card' or *carte* was first used of playing-cards.

carol was originally used to mean a kind of dance, the word coming from the Old French word *carole*. This in turn came from the Latin *corolla* 'a garland'. The dance was accompanied by music, and later the word was applied to the music itself.

cashier comes from the French *caissier*, from *casse* meaning money-chest.

castanet has come into English from Spanish as *castañeta*, which in turn comes from the Latin word *castanea* 'chestnut'. Castanets are so-called because of their shape, which resembles a chestnut.

chameleon is a Latin word taken from Greek *chamaileon*. *Chamai* means 'on (or near) the ground' (a dwarf), and *leon* is 'lion'. So the word means 'dwarf lion', although a chameleon is not, of course, a lion at all.

chap once meant 'a customer or purchaser', and is taken from 'chapman' meaning 'a dealer'. In its other sense 'chap' is related to 'chip' and 'chop', the sort of blow which causes a crack.

church comes from Greek, and in English once had a sound like 'k' instead of 'ch'. In Scotland the word 'kirk' is still used. Its origin is in the Greek word *kyrios* 'lord'; so it means 'house of the Lord'.

cliché is a French word, first used in the 19th century for the metal printing block called a 'stereotype plate'. The word *clicher* described the sound made as the mould was dropped into the molten metal. It then came to be used to describe any commonplace phrase, word or idea.

clove If you look closely at a clove it looks very like a nail. The English name comes from the French *clou de girofle* 'nail of the clove-tree'.

clumsy is of Scandinavian origin, where it has several meanings. *Klumsen* means 'to strike dumb' or 'hamper' and also 'dazed, numb'. Its meaning has changed in English.

CHAMELION

COLONEL

coach comes from a place-name in Hungary called Kocs (pronounced 'koch'). It was here that the *Kocsi szekér* (Kocs cart) was invented in the 15th century. The word has passed into most European languages, pronounced much as in English.

colonel is connected with the word 'column', being the officer who led such a column. Some languages spelled the word 'coronel', which explains why in English it has an unusual pronunciation.

companion is from French *compagnon*. This is taken from the Latin *com* 'with' and *panis* 'bread', producing a word which means 'one who eats bread with another'.

comrade really means 'chamber-fellow', since it comes from the Latin root *camera*, meaning 'chamber' or 'room'.

In French it is *camarade*, and in Spanish *camarada*, both meaning · 'room-mate'.

confetti comes from Italian and means 'small sweets'. Traditionally sweets were thrown after weddings, and later small discs of paper were used.

constable is from the Latin *comes stabuli*, which means 'officer in charge of the stable'. Governors of royal castles in England and France were given the title 'constable', which was first used to mean 'an officer of the peace' in the 14th century.

copper was, in ancient times, found mostly on the island of Cyprus. The metal took its name *copreum* from the island, whose Latin name was *Cyprium* or *Cuprium*.

cosy is a word of Scottish origin which is possibly connected with the Norwegian word *koselig* 'snug, cosy'. The word in English was once spelled 'colsie'.

cot is a word adopted from India, where it takes the form in Hindi of *khat*, meaning a 'bedstead, couch or hammock'. Such a bed was first used by British soldiers in India, and the word was brought back home by them in about the 17th century.

crane is a bird from which a machine takes its name. Many other animals have given their names to mechanical objects, for example, monkey-wrench, donkey-engine, kite and pig-iron.

crimson takes its name from an insect, the *kermes*, which was once used for making a red dye. The kermes was also known in Spanish and Italian as *cremesin* and *cremesino*, and it was from these that the English word came.

crook is used to describe 'swindlers' or 'criminals' because they are 'not straight'. It is also possible that our word 'crooked' comes from the Old Norse *krokottr* 'crooked, winding, cunning or wily'.

crusade comes from the French *crois* 'cross', and also from the Spanish *cruzar* 'to take up the cross'.

crypt comes from the Greek, meaning 'a vault', but the root of the same word also means 'hidden'. So in English we have 'cryptic' meaning 'hidden, secret', and 'cryptogram' which is a secret message in code.

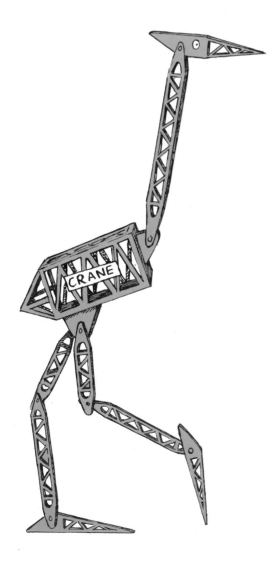

currant takes its name from Corinth, in Greece, which was the place from which currants were first sent abroad. The name came into English from France, where the fruit was originally called *raisin de Coraunte*, or 'Corinth grape'.

dahlia is a flower which was named in 1791 in honour of the Swedish botanist Anders Dahl.

damson is taken from the word *damascene*, since this fruit was originally called the damascene plum or 'plum of Damascus'. The fruit was first cultivated in Syria, and so takes its name from its capital.

dean has come to English through Latin from Greek. The word was originally *dekanos*, the name given to a monk or other dignitary in charge of ten others. In Greek *deka* means 'ten'.

decoy comes from the Dutch *de kooieend* 'the duck decoy'. The word *kooi* in Dutch means 'cage'.

deer originally meant any kind of wild animal. Dutch and German still use the words *dier* and *tier* to mean 'animal'.

denarius is the shortened form of *denarius nummus*, a Roman coin containing ten *asses*. The letter 'd' was formerly used in Britain to denote a penny.

denim takes its name from the place where it was made in the 17th century: Nîmes in France. In French, it was known as *serge de Nîmes*.

9

derrick has a rather gruesome origin, since it takes its name from the gallows on which criminals were hanged. In about 1600 the surname of the hangman at Tyburn, near London, was Derrick and he gave his name to the gallows there.

diesel takes its name from the inventor of the diesel engine. Rudolf Diesel was a German engineer who patented his engine in 1893, although he never made his fortune from it. He died at the age of 55 after falling overboard from the Antwerp to Harwich steamer.

dinner comes from the French *dîner*, and its earlier form *disner*. This came from the Latin *disjejunare* 'to break fast'. In fact, the French word *déjeuner* 'to breakfast' also comes from the same Latin word.

dinosaur is a word invented in 1841 to describe certain prehistoric animals. It is made up of two Greek words, *deinos* meaning 'terrible' and *sauros* 'lizard', which produces the description 'terrible lizard'.

dismal originally meant 'evil days', referring to so-called 'unlucky' days in the medieval calendar. The word comes from the Latin *dies mali* 'evil days', which became *dis mal* in Norman French, and one word in English.

dollar is a form of the German word *taler* or *thaler*. This is a shortening of 'Joachimsthaler', the name of a silver coin made in about 1518 from metal found in Joachimsthal (Joachim's valley), in Bohemia, in the west of Czechoslovakia. The Spanish eight reales coin was commonly called a dollar, and was used in the 'New World'.

domino The name of the game dominoes probably comes from the Italian exclamation *domino!* meaning 'master' or 'winner'.

dreary comes from the Old English word *dreor*, meaning 'gore, flowing with blood'. Its meaning has slowly changed since the early days.

dromedary literally means 'a fast runner', from the Greek word *dromad*.

10

dunce comes from the name of John Duns Scotus, who was far from being a dunce. The word was applied contemptuously to the followers of Scotus in the 14th century by those who opposed his ideas and ridiculed his teachings.

E

earwig is so called because in early times it was thought (quite wrongly) that the insects could penetrate the ear. The same ideas occur in French (*perce-oreille* 'pierce-ear'), German and Dutch, (*Ohrwurm* and *oorworm* 'ear-worm').

elastic was first used to describe expansion in substances such as gases. It comes from the Greek *elastikos*, meaning 'driving' or 'propelling'. Later, it came to mean 'to resume normal size after expansion'.

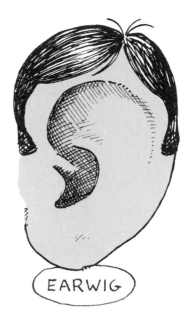

EARWIG

electricity comes from the Greek name for amber, *elektron*. This is because amber can be given an electric charge and made to attract small pieces of materials such as paper and cotton after being rubbed.

embargo is a Spanish word and comes from the verb *embargar*, meaning 'to arrest or impede'. An embargo was an order forbidding any ships to leave or enter a harbour, usually when a war was declared.

engine today means a mechanical contrivance, but it once meant 'wit' or 'genius'. It is related to the word 'ingenious', and so also meant 'cleverness'. The idea of an engine being a machine came into the English language in about the 14th century.

evangelist strictly means 'one who brings good tidings'. An angel brought messages from God, but especially good news was carried by an *evangel*. In later times evangelism has come to mean the teaching or preaching of the gospel.

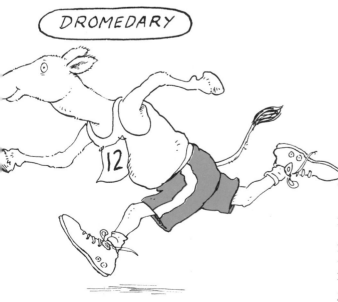

DROMEDARY

12

exhilarate comes from the same root as 'hilarious'. This word comes from the Latin *ex* 'out of' and *hilarare* 'to cheer', giving an original meaning 'bringing out happiness'.

explode is a word which has changed its meaning. It came from the Latin *explodere* and originally meant 'to drive out by clapping', or, in the theatre 'to hiss off the stage'.

F

fad dates from the 19th century, and is a shortening of the earlier expression 'fidfad'. This in turn was a shortening of 'fiddle-faddle', a 16th-century term meaning 'trifling talk or action'.

fan is simply an abbreviation of 'fanatic', someone who has a frenzied manner, and particularly who is madly devoted to an idea. The present meaning of the word 'fan' entered English in the United States in the 19th century.

FERRET

SWAG

ferret comes from a Latin word *fur* meaning 'thief', probably because the animal invades the burrows of other creatures. The same root-word is found in the word 'furtive'.

fiasco is the Italian word for 'bottle' or 'flask'. When something goes wrong, an Italian might say 'it has made a bottle', but no-one quite knows why this expression is used.

flabbergast is a made-up word which was first used in the 18th century. It is made up of the word 'flabby' or 'flap', joined to the word 'aghast'.

flour and **flower** both come from the French word *fleur*. In the first word, the French expression was *fleur de farine* or 'flower of wheat'. The spelling 'flower' for both meanings was quite common in English until the early 19th century.

focus is the Latin word for 'fireplace', the central point in a room. It was also used to describe a 'burning-point', such as when a lens was used for focusing the rays of the sun to burn something.

foreign is from the French *forain*, which comes from the Latin *foranus* 'a foreigner'. This in turn is taken from the Latin word *foris* 'outside'.

fortnight is a shortening of 'fourteen nights', as in medieval times periods were reckoned by nights rather than days. There was also an old word *sennight*, meaning 'seven nights', or 'a week'.

franchise originally meant 'freedom', and comes from the Old French *franche* 'free'. It came to have its present meaning (the right to vote) during the 18th century. Before that it meant 'privilege or immunity under the law'.

A LOOSELY FITTING UPPER GARMENT

G

gaberdine (also spelled *gabardine*) is a type of cloth, but also gave its name to a loosely fitting upper garment.

galvanize takes its name from the Italian scientist, Luigi Galvani, who discovered this process of producing electricity by chemical action in 1792.

gas is a word invented in the 17th century by the Dutch chemist J.B. van Helmont, who took the name from the Greek word *chaos* meaning 'atmosphere'. The Greek 'ch' sound is a guttural one and is represented in Dutch by the letter 'g'.

gingham is taken from the Malay word *ginggang*, which meant 'striped' and was applied to cloth which had stripes. It was used by Dutch traders in the East Indies in the 17th century, and passed onto English and other languages.

glamour once meant 'magic', or 'spell', but by the 19th century had come to mean 'magic beauty', largely due to its use by the Scottish writer, Sir Walter Scott. It is from a 15th-century Scottish word *gramarye* formed from the word 'grammar', meaning 'magic learning'.

gooseberry has nothing to do with the goose, but comes from *groose* which is related to the German word *kraus*, meaning 'curly'. In French it is called *groseille*, and in medieval Latin the plant was known as *uva crispa*, or 'curly grape'.

grapefruit is a word which came into English through the United States. It is so called because the fruit grows in clusters, like giant bunches of grapes. It is also known as the 'pomelo', while an earlier form of the fruit was called the 'shaddock', named from a Captain Shaddock who introduced the fruit to Jamaica from the East Indies.

grenade comes from the French word *grenade*, meaning a 'pomegranate'. The name was applied to this explosive shell because of its resemblance to the fruit. In Old French, the fruit was called *pome grenade*.

grocer originally meant 'a dealer in the gross', or a 'wholesaler'. In London, the Grocers' Company was a group of people who dealt largely in foreign produce, which gave the word its modern sense.

guinea pig has nothing to do with the African country of Guinea, nor does it refer to a pig. The name 'Guinea' was often used vaguely for 'distant country', and the word 'pig' equally as imprecisely for an animal. It is also called the 'cavy'.

HARMONICA
or
MOUTH ORGAN

H

halibut means 'holy fish', the word *butt* being an old Dutch word for all kinds of flat fish. It was so called because it was eaten on holy days. Another name containing a form of *butt* is turbot, meaning 'thorn-fish'.

hamburger is named after the German city of Hamburg. The full expression is 'Hamburger steak', meaning 'steak in the Hamburg style'.

handsome originally meant 'easy or pleasant to handle'. Its meaning was extended to mean 'pleasant', and then 'of pleasing appearance'. It still retains its other meaning of 'ample, sizeable or large'.

harmonica was first used by Benjamin Franklin in 1762 to describe a glass musical instrument. Nowadays it is used as a name for the mouth organ, an instrument dating back to the early 19th century, then called the 'aura'.

hazard is a word which started as the name of a game of dice, but later extended to all kinds of risks. The word comes to English from French *hasard*, through Spanish *azar*. The Spaniards adopted the word from the Arabic word *az-zahr*, meaning a gaming die.

hearse comes from the French word *herse*, describing a triangular iron frame used in church to hold candles. The candle-holder was placed over the coffin in church, and the name was later applied to the frame or canopy containing the coffin, set up in the church or carried through the streets.

helicopter is a modern word made up of two Greek ones: *heliko* meaning 'screw' and *pteron* meaning 'wing'.

hieroglyphic comes from the Greek words *hieros* 'sacred' and *glyphe* 'writing'. The word is found in the writings of th Greek philosopher Plutarch (AD 46–119), meaning 'letters or writing', but it was also used in the 16th century to describe secret or symbolic writing.

hippopotamus is a word taken from the Greek *hippos* 'horse' and *potamos* 'river', although the animal is not related to the horse.

hooligan comes from the name of a rowdy Irish family, called Houlihan, who lived in Southwark in south-east London in the late 19th century. The family was immortalized by a music-hall song popular at the time.

host comes from the Old French *hoste* (now *hôte*), meaning a host or guest, from the Latin *hospes*. The English words 'hotel' and 'hostel' come from the same source.

humble comes from the Latin, meaning 'lowly' or 'mean'. But the phrase 'to eat humble-pie' has quite a different origin. It comes from 'umbles', the cheaply-bought inner parts of an animal.

husband is a word which once applied to all men who were masters of the household, whether married or not. The word comes from the Old Norse *husbondi* meaning 'someone who has a household'.

I

idiot once meant simply 'an ignorant person' or 'peasant', and comes from the Greek *idiotes*, meaning a common person or layman.

illustrate originally meant to 'throw light upon', and still retains that meaning in some senses. It had nothing to do with pictures until the 17th century.

indigo is a blue powder dye obtained from the plant *Indigofera*. In the 16th and 17th centuries it was spelled *indico*, having been taken from the Spanish. It comes originally from the Greek *Indikos*, meaning 'of India'.

infantry once applied to a force of soldiers who were too young to serve in the cavalry. It comes from the Italian *infante* meaning a 'boy'. It was only in the 16th century that the word was applied to all foot-soldiers.

insulate comes from the Latin word *insula* meaning 'island', expressing the idea 'to isolate or detach'. Since about 1800 the word has taken on the specific meaning 'to prevent the passage of electricity'.

interfere In the 16th century this word was used about horses and meant 'to strike the fetlock with the hoof of the opposite foot', or 'to knock one leg against the other'. It later came to mean 'to collide or clash', and since the 18th century, 'to intervene'. The word comes from France.

interlude was originally used to describe a short play, dance or piece of music performed in the middle of a longer entertainment. It comes from the Latin *inter* 'between' and *ludus* 'play'.

intoxicate has changed its meaning since the 16th century, when it simply meant 'to poison'. The word comes from the Greek *toxikon* a 'poison for arrows', from the related word *toxon* a 'bow'.

INFANT-RY

J

jacket comes from the French *jacquette*, which in turn comes from *jacque*. It is also the personal name Jacques, but in the common use meant a leather jerkin or a leather drinking vessel. In English it was spelled 'jack' or 'jacket'.

jazz is of uncertain origin, but is certainly from a North American source. It is considered possible that it came from Chas (a shortening of Charles), the name of a Black musician.

jeans comes from the name of the fabric used, and is short for 'jean fustian'. It was formerly spelled 'jenes' or 'geanes', from *Gênes*, a French spelling of the city of Genoa which is where the cloth was first made.

jeopardy takes its name from chess, and refers to a divided game – one for which the outcome cannot be foreseen and is therefore uncertain. The Spanish expression for this is *juego de partido* and in French *jeu parti*. The English word comes from this.

jockey is a pet form of the name Jock, which is a Scottish variety of the name Jack. In the 16th century the word jockey meant simply 'lad', but later it came to mean a 'horse-dealer' and then a 'horse-rider'.

jubilee is of Hebrew origin, and refers to a year of celebration kept every 50 years. The word comes from *yobel*, a 'ram's horn'. This is because jubilee year was proclaimed by blowing upon a ram's horn.

jumper comes from the word 'jump', which had nothing to do with leaping up and down. It meant a man's short coat or a woman's bodice, and came from an Arabic word meaning a garment such as a skirt.

K

ketchup is a word of Malay or Chinese origin. It is certainly from the Far East, since the word in Malay is *kechap*, and in Amoy Chinese it is *ke-tsiap* meaning a 'sauce of fish'. It reached English through Dutch.

JUMPER

kidnap comes from the slang word for a child 'kid', and 'nap' an earlier form of 'nab'. It was originally used in the United States to describe someone who stole children to provide cheap labourers and servants for the plantations.

kite is an old English word and comes from the Anglo-Saxon *cyta*, which is the name of a bird of prey.

knickers is an abbreviation taken from the name Diedrich Knickerbocker, the supposed author of Washington Irving's *History of New York*. The illustrations showed characters wearing baggy knee-breeches which became known as 'knickerbockers'.

lacrosse is a French word which came into English through the French settlers in North America. The full name of the game is *le jeu de la crosse*, meaning 'the game of the crooked stick'. The word *crosse* probably comes from the German, meaning 'crutch'.

launch The word for a type of boat, comes from a quite different source from the verb 'to launch'. A launch derives from the Portuguese, who took it from the Malayan word *lanchar*, meaning 'quick' or 'nimble'. The second meaning 'to launch' comes from the word 'lance' which is a kind of spear.

ledger originally meant a book which lies permanently in one place. The word comes from an Old English root, meaning 'lay' or 'lie'.

lens takes its name from the lentil vegetable, for which the Latin name is *lens*. The reason for this is that the curved glass of a lens is shaped something like a lentil. It was first used in the 17th century.

lettuce comes from the French word *laitue*, which in turn is taken from the Latin *lactuca*. The *lact* part of the word means 'milk', used because of the milky juice of the plant.

library comes from the Latin word *libraria*, meaning a bookseller's shop. The French still use the word *librairie* in the same way.

linoleum was a trade name for a patent taken out by F. Walton in 1860 for a floor covering using linen (flax) and oil. The word is a compound of the Latin words *linum* 'flax' and *oleum* 'oil'.

lobster comes from the Anglo-Saxon word *loppestre*. This comes either from *loppe* meaning 'spider' or from the earlier word *lopust*, which by some mispronunciation comes from the Latin *locusta* meaning 'locust'.

locomotive was first used in the 17th century. It was taken from the Latin phrase *in loco moveri* 'to move by change of position in space'.

ludo is simply the Latin for 'I play', the game being a modification of the old Persian game of Pachesi, introduced into Britain in 1896.

lunch is not a shortening of 'luncheon'. In fact, the second word is a lengthening of the first. The idea was based on the English dialect word 'nuncheon', meaning 'a draught taken at noon'.

M

margarine was invented in about 1860 by the French chemist Mèges-Mouriès. He believed that his product consisted mainly of margaric acid, discovered earlier by Chevreul. The acid formed globules like pearls, and the name was taken from the Greek *margarites* 'pearl'.

mascot comes from the Italian word *masca* 'witch'. In the form *mascotto* 'little witch', it passed into other languages, reaching English through the French *mascotte*, by which time it had begun to mean a 'good luck charm'.

mayonnaise takes its name from the capital of Minorca, Port Mahón. The sauce was named *mahonnaise* in honour of the capture of the town from the English by the French Duc de Richelieu in 1756.

mesmerize is named after one of the earliest people to practise hypnotism, the Austrian physician Friedrich Anton Mesmer (1733–1815).

migraine is the French form of the older word *megrim*, which is taken from the Greek *hemikrania* 'half-skull', because the illness affects only one side of the head.

minaret is from the Spanish word *minarete*. This in turn was taken from the Turkish word *minare*, which again came from the Arabic *manarat*. Even this word comes from another Arabic word, *manar* meaning 'lighthouse'. The final part of this word *nar* means 'fire'.

mob is an abbreviation of 'mobile', taken from the Latin expression *mobile vulgus* 'the excitable or fickle crowd'. It began as a slang expression in the 17th century, and was gradually adopted into standard English.

magazine is from an Arabic word *makhazin* which is the plural form of the word *makhzan*, meaning 'storehouse'. This word describes a place where guns and arms are stored, and a receptacle for bullets. In the 17th century the word was used to mean a 'storehouse of information', leading to its present meaning.

magnolia is a flower named after Pierre Magnol (1638–1715) who was professor of botany at Montpellier, France.

malaria was once believed to have been caused by the 'bad air' given off in marshy places. It was therefore named in Italy as *mal'aria*, the short form of *mala aria*, meaning 'bad air'.

map is taken from the Latin expression *mappa mundi*, meaning 'sheet of the world'. In classical Latin, the word *mappa* meant 'table-cloth'.

money comes from the temple of the goddess Juno in Rome which was called Moneta – one of Juno's other titles. The Roman mint was housed in a building adjoining this temple, and the mint became known as the *moneta*. From this word came the English words 'money' and 'mint'.

monster originally meant a misshapen creature, not necessarily a large one. By the 16th century it also meant something large. The word comes from the Latin *monstrum*, meaning 'something marvellous or wonderful'.

mosquito is a Spanish and Portuguese word and means simply 'little fly'. This comes from the Latin word *musca* 'fly'.

moustache came into English from French, but other languages have a similar word, for example the Italian *mostaccio* and Spanish *mostacho*. All these come from the Greek word *mastax*, meaning 'jaw'.

mummy came to English through French and Spanish, but its origin is the Arabic word *mumiya*, meaning 'an embalmed body'. *Mum* is the Arabic word for the wax used in the preserving process.

navy is a word of Latin origin, from *navis* 'a ship'.

newt is a word changed by being mispronounced. It was originally *ewt*, and when referred to as 'an ewt' confusion led to the 'n' being tacked onto the second word. 'Ewt' comes from the early words 'evet' and 'eft', from the Anglo-Saxon *efete*.

nightingale means 'singer of the night', and is taken from the Anglo-Saxon word *nihtegale. Niht* means 'night' and *gale* is 'singer'.

nostalgia comes from the Greek *nostos* 'return home' and *algos* 'pain'. Together they produce the meaning of 'homesickness'.

oboe comes from the French word *hautbois*, which has the same meaning. The French word is pronounced *oh-bwah*, and the English word is an imitation of this.

ocean comes into English from the Old French word *occean*, taken from the Greek *okeanos*. This word was used to describe the 'great river' which was believed to encircle the world. The names of the present oceans have been formed in various ways. The Atlantic Ocean takes its name from Atlas, the Titan in Greek mythology who was believed to hold up the pillars of the universe. The Mediterranean (strictly, of course, a sea) is the English form of the Latin *Mare Mediterraneum* which means 'sea in the centre of the land'. The Pacific Ocean was named *Mare Pacificum* by the Portuguese explorer Magellan, because he found it peaceful and free of storms. The Arctic Ocean derives its name from its northern position. The North, or Pole Star, is in the constellation of the Great Bear, and so is called *arktos* in Greek, meaning 'bear'. 'Antarctic' simply means 'opposite to the Arctic'.

ogre comes from the French, and is found in the *Fairy Stories* of Perrault, published in 1697. The word is found nowhere else and it is possible that Perrault himself invented it, although there is a Latin word *orcus*, meaning 'infernal deity'.

oratorio is the Italian form of the word 'oratory', a place of prayer. In the 16th century musical performances were held at the oratory of St Philip Neri in Rome, and so the Italian word *oratorio* was applied to all such performances.

ounce comes from the Latin *uncia* which means a twelfth part of a pound, or the twelfth part of an inch. (In troy weight, there are 12 ounces to a pound.) The word 'inch' also comes from the same Latin word.

ozone comes from the Greek *ozein*, meaning 'smell'. It was named by the scientist C.F. Schonbein in 1840 because of its peculiar smell.

pagoda comes from the Persian word *butkada. But* means 'idol' or 'god', and *kada* is a 'house' or 'habitation'. The whole word has the meaning 'idol-house'.

pal comes from the gypsy word *pral* or *phral* meaning 'brother'. The gypsies came from India, and the ancient Indian language, Sanskrit, also has the word *bhratri* meaning 'brother'.

pants is an abbreviation of the word 'pantaloons'. This word comes from the Italian *pantalone*, which was the name used for a stock Venetian comedy character who always wore baggy trousers.

paper comes from the French *papier* which, in turn, is taken from the Latin *papyros* and the Greek *papyrus* – the reed-like plant originally used by the Ancient Egyptians for writing on.

parakeet comes from the Spanish *periquito* and the Old French, *paroquet* also meaning 'parrot'.

pawn The two meanings of this word come from quite separate sources. The name of the chess piece comes through French from the Spanish *peon* and Italian *pedone* 'footman', and originally from the Persian *piyadah* 'foot soldier'. The meaning 'pawn' as 'something held as security' also comes from Old French; *pan* meaning 'pledge' or 'plunder'.

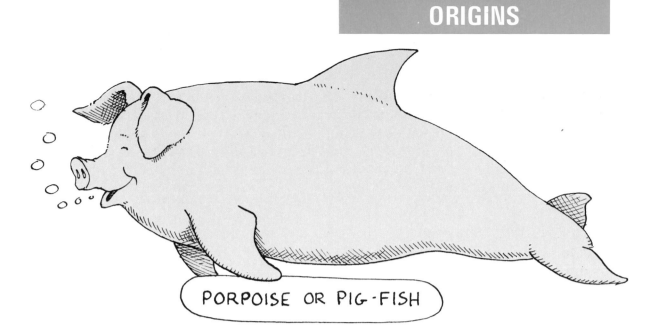

PORPOISE OR PIG-FISH

pea is an example of a word formed from a 'false plural'. The word was originally 'pease', but people thought that it was a plural, and the ending was dropped to form *pea*. The old word is still in use in such expressions as 'pease pudding'. It is derived from the Latin word *piza*, in turn from Greek *pison*.

pepper is a word which goes right back to the ancient Sanskrit language, where it appears as *pippali*. It appears in most European languages with slightly different spellings: *pfeffer* (German), *poivre* (French) and *piper* (Latin).

petrol is the shorter form of the word 'petroleum', formed from the Latin *petra oleum*, meaning 'rock oil'.

piano is an abbreviation of *pianoforte*, which is an Italian word coming from the phrase *gravecembalo di piano e forte*, meaning 'harpsichord with soft and loud'. This description was used by the inventor Bartolomeo Cristofori in about 1710.

pilot reached English from the French *pilote*, through the Medieval Latin word *pilotus*. This in turn was taken from the Greek *pedon*, which means 'an oar' or 'a rudder'.

plagiarize originally described something far worse than its present meaning. Plagiary was kidnapping, and the word comes from the Latin *plagium* meaning 'man-stealing'.

plebiscite is of Latin origin, the first part referring to the *plebs*, who were the common people of Rome. The ending is formed from *scitum*, meaning 'law'. So the whole word refers to a law made by the common people.

pluck In modern slang English, people are referred to as having 'guts', meaning they are courageous. 'Pluck' has a similar origin. It is the act of plucking out the heart, liver and lungs from the carcass of an animal. The meaning 'to pull out' comes from the Anglo-Saxon word *pluccian*.

poker The name of the game, poker, entered English in the United States from the German *pochspiel*, which was a 'bluffing' card-game. The German word *pochen* means 'to brag or to thrust'.

porpoise comes from the Latin *porcus* 'pig' and *piscis* 'fish', suggesting that the animal is a 'pig-fish'; not true zoologically, but a fairly apt description.

21

portcullis comes from the Old French *port coleïce*. The first word means 'door', while the second means 'sliding or gliding'.

pound comes from the Latin word *pondo*, which is the source of the meanings in English referring to weight and money. There was originally a pound weight of silver in the English pound.

pram is short for 'perambulator'. The word perambulate means 'to walk' or 'to travel', and comes from a similar Latin word. A perambulator was once a person who travelled, but was first used to describe a baby-carriage in the 19th century.

precipice once meant a 'headlong fall', but by the 17th century it had taken on its present meaning. It comes from the Latin *praecipitium*, formed from *praeceps* 'headlong, steep'.

prestige comes from the French, and originally from the Latin *praestigium*, meaning 'illusion'. It referred to the tricks used by a juggler, and 'prestigitation' still means 'performing conjuring tricks'. The modern meaning suggests 'brilliance or glamour from past successes'.

problem is from the French *problème*, taken from the Latin *problema*. This is directly from the Greek, formed from *proballein*. *Pro* means 'before, earlier' and *ballein* 'throw'.

propaganda is a word taken from the Church, and originally meant a committee of cardinals charged with foreign missions. It comes from the Latin *propagare* 'to muliltiply specimens' (such as a plant), or 'to increase or spread'.

pterodactyl is a recent word made up from Greek roots. *Pteron* means 'wing' and *daktulos* is 'finger'. This reptile's wings are formed from an extension of the front claws or 'fingers'.

pulpit comes from the Latin *pulpitum*, meaning 'a raised structure, stage or scaffold'. The French word for 'desk' *pupitre* comes from the same source.

pygmy is a word of Greek origin. The original word was *pugmaios*, meaning 'dwarfish' or 'very small'. It is taken from another Greek word *pugme* 'fist' which is also a measure of length, from the elbow to the knuckles.

quarantine is from the Medieval Latin *quadrantena*, and refers to a period of 40 days. Originally it was the legal period that a widow was allowed to remain in her late husband's house, but the present meaning came into use in about the 17th century.

quicksilver means 'living silver', from the fact that the metal runs when poured. This uses an old meaning of 'quick', in the sense of 'live'.

raisin Although it means 'a dried grape' in English, this word in some other languages simply means 'grape'. It comes from the Latin *racemus* 'a cluster of grapes'.

ramshackle was once spelled and pronounced 'ranshackle', since it was a variation of the word 'ransack'. 'Ransack' comes from an Old Norse word *rannsaka*, meaning 'to search for stolen goods'. *Rann* means 'house' and *saka* means 'seek'.

rebel comes from the French *rebelle* and Latin *rebellis*. This comes from *re* 'again', and *bellum* 'war'. The word 'revel' comes from the same source, originally meaning 'to rejoice noisily' and 'to make a disturbance'.

reckless is formed from the words 'reck' and 'less'. 'Reck' means 'to take care, heed, or concern oneself'. It is an Anglo-Saxon word, spelled 'reccan'. 'Reckless' appears in Dutch as *roekeloos* and German as *ruchlos*.

reindeer is an Old Norse word, *hreindyri*, and it is from this that the English word is derived. The word appears in other European languages in different spellings: *rendier* (Dutch), *renntier* (German) or simply *renne* (French).

repair comes from the French *réparer*, and in turn from the Latin *reparare*. This uses the prefix *re* 'go back to an earlier state', plus *parare* 'to make ready, or put in order'.

republic comes from two Latin words, *res* 'affair or thing' and *publica* 'public'. The word originally was *respublica*, but the 's' was dropped in French, which is the source of the English word.

restaurant is a French word taken from the verb *restaurer* 'to restore', and the word was originally used to mean 'a food which restores'. The modern use comes from an eating-house called a *restaurant* which opened in Paris in 1765.

rhinoceros comes from the Greek *rhin-* 'nose' and *keras* 'horn', forming into a word meaning 'nose-horn'. There have been several ways of making a plural of the word ('rhinocerotes', 'rhinocerons', 'rhinocerontes'), but nowadays the correct plural is 'rhinoceroses'.

robot comes from the Czech word *robota* meaning 'compulsory service', but first acquired its modern meaning when Karel Capek used it to mean 'mechanical slave' in his play *R.U.R.* in 1921. In Russian (a language related to Czech), the word *rabota* means 'work, labour'.

ROBOT
OR
MECHANICAL SLAVE

23

rosemary was, until about the 14th century, known as *rosmarine*, a word which comes from the Latin *ros marinus* meaning 'sea-dew'.

ruffian has nothing to do with the word 'rough', but comes from the Italian word *ruffiano*, taken from an older word *roffia* 'beastly thing'.

ADOLPHE SAX

salary is from the Latin *salarium*, in turn from the word *sal* 'salt'. This is because a salary was originally money given to Roman soldiers to buy salt. Later it came to mean any kind of pay.

sandwich is a word taken from a name. John Montagu, the 11th Earl of Sandwich (1718–92), was so fond of gambling that he was reluctant to get up from the table for a meal. Instead he asked for meat to be served between two slices of bread.

sarcophagus is from the Greek *sarko* 'flesh' and *phagos* 'eating', meaning 'flesh-eating'. This was because the Ancient Greeks believed that the stone used could actually swallow up the corpse and the wooden coffin.

saucer was originally simply a small dish on which sauce was served. The word 'sauce' comes from the Latin *salsa*, meaning 'salted'. The same article is called *soucoupe* in French and *sottocoppa* in Italian, both meaning 'an under-cup'.

saxophone is named after Adolphe Sax, a Belgian who invented the instrument in 1842. He also invented the saxhorn and the saxotromba.

scarlet was originally the name of a rich cloth, which was often bright red, but could also be various other colours. English took it from the Old French *escarlate* or Italian *scarlatto*. In turn, these words come from the Persian word *saqirlat* 'broadcloth'.

schooner is a word from North America. The word was sometimes spelled 'scooner', and was applied to a ship first built at Gloucester, Massachusetts in about 1713. It is probably derived from the verb 'to scon' meaning 'to send skimming over the water'.

scout originally meant 'to spy', and comes from the Old French word *escouter* 'to listen'. The Latin form is *auscultare*. So 'a scout' is someone sent out to spy or reconnoitre.

seal, in the sense of a closure, comes from the Old French *seel*, in turn taken from the Latin *sigillum* meaning 'a small picture' as well as 'seal'. The name of the animal comes from the Anglo-Saxon *seolh*.

semaphore is from Greek *sema* 'signal' and *phoros* 'bearing', a word invented in about 1812 in France, and adopted into English.

sentry is a corruption of the word 'sanctuary'. This was a place of safety, and was later applied to a shelter for a watchman, and then to the watchman himself.

shack is a word from Central America and comes from the Mexican *jacal*, and in turn from the Aztec word *xacatli*, meaning a 'wooden hut'.

shanty has a similar meaning to 'shack' and comes from North America. It is a corruption of the French word *chantier*, meaning 'a workshop'. In North America it had the special meaning of 'a hut used by woodcutters'.

shawl is a word of Eastern origin. In Persian the word is *shal*, and similar words are found in Indian languages. With varying spellings the word is found in most European languages.

sheriff is an old English word, coming from the Anglo-Saxon *scirgerefa*, or 'shire-reeve'. 'Shire' refers to a county and 'reeve' was a local official.

shilling is a word found in most European languages, yet its origin is uncertain. In German it is *schilling*, in Norwegian *skilling*, in Old French and Spanish *escalin*, and in Italian *scellino*.

shirt comes from the same source as 'skirt', which is the Old Norse word *skyrta* 'shirt'. Exactly how this word came to mean two different things is not clear. In German there is another similar word *schürze*, meaning 'apron'.

shuffle comes from the German *schuffeln*, and is connected with such

ETIENNE DE SILHOUETTE

words as 'scuffle' and 'shove', all with the meaning of pushing along, putting together, or thrusting.

silhouette is named after a French politician, Etienne de Silhouette (1704–67), who is said to have been so mean that in his home he would not have fully-executed drawings, but only outlines, in order to save money.

sinister comes from the Latin, and simply means 'left' or 'to the left'. The left was associated with bad omens, while the right was favoured. The Latin word for 'right' is *dexter*, giving rise to the English 'dexterity', meaning 'skill or adroitness'.

sir is a short form of sire, a word used for people of rank. It comes from the French which, in earlier times, had *sieur*, from *seigneur*. This came from Latin *senior*. More complicated forms are *monseigneur* and *monsieur* 'my sir'. Italian also has the word *monsignor*.

skipper is from the Dutch *schipper*, from the word *schip* 'ship'. The English word 'equip' is from the same source. In early France the word for 'boarding ship' was taken from the Dutch, becoming *eskip* or *esquip*. The 's' was dropped, forming the word 'equip' which has, over the years, changed its meaning.

slave comes from the Latin word *Sclavus*, meaning 'Slav', one of the peoples of Eastern Europe, such as the Russians, the Poles or Bulgarians. They had been conquered and made to serve as slaves, so the word became adapted to mean any person owned by another.

slot is of Germanic origin, and is still found in German as *schloss*, meaning 'lock', 'clasp' or 'castle'. Its original meaning in English was 'bar' or 'rod' rather than 'an opening', since it was used for bolting or locking.

smart was once used only in the sense of a sharp, stinging pain. It had the same meaning in Old English, and only in the 12th century did it come to mean 'brisk, vigorous', and later still 'clever'. The meaning of 'well-dressed' dates from the early 18th century.

smug originally meant 'trim', 'neat' or 'smooth'. From 'sleek' the meaning changed in the 19th century to 'self-satisfied'. It is probably related to the German word *schmücken* 'to adorn'.

sock originally meant 'shoe' or 'light slipper', coming from the Latin word *soccus*. Later it meant any covering for the foot and then came to mean, as it does today, a short stocking.

soldier strictly means 'someone serving in an army for pay', since the word has its origins in the Latin word *solidus* 'a gold coin'. This word changed as it was used in Portuguese and Spanish into *sueldo* and *soldo*, both names of coins and also the word for 'pay'. So a soldier was one who was paid in such coins. In France, the five-centime coin was called *sou*.

soybean is a combination of 'soya' and 'bean'. 'Soya' comes to English from the Dutch form *soja* taken from Malay *soi*. This came from the Japanese *sho-yu* and Chinese *shi-yau*, formed from *shi* 'salted beans' and *yu* 'oil'.

spaghetti is an Italian word, formed as a plural of *spaghetto*. This is taken from the word *spago*, meaning 'cord'. So the whole word means 'little cords'.

spell originally comes from a Germanic word meaning 'magic formula' and is still used in that sense. But it was also borrowed by the French, who used it to mean 'explain', and later to 'spell' words.

spider was *spithre* in Anglo-Saxon, where it had the meaning of 'spinner'. In fact, early forms of English did refer to the spider as 'spinner'.

spinach comes from the Latin word *spina*, since some varieties of the plant have prickly seeds. But it is possible that the Latin word was taken from a Persian name for spinach, *aspanakh*.

sport is an English word which has been adopted by many other languages in the world. It comes from the verb disport 'to divert, play or frolic', and originally meant any kind of pleasant pastime.

squat comes from the Old French *esquatir* 'to press flat'. Later the word changed to *quatir*, and in the form *se*

MAN AND SUPERMAN

quatir meant 'to crouch'. It came into English in the 15th century.

star is of Anglo-Saxon origin, but the same root exists in many European languages. The Latin word was *stella* (from which comes the English word 'stellar'), and the Greek was *aster* (from which comes the English words 'asteroid' and 'astronaut'). In German it is *stern*, and in Italian *stella*.

steeple comes from the Anglo-Saxon *stepel* 'a tall tower', and is related to the word 'steep'. A horse-race known as a steeplechase is so called because originally the riders used a distant steeple as a landmark and goal.

sterling originally referred to a silver penny used in England in Norman times. It seems likely that the word arose from Anglo-Saxon *steorling*, from *steorra* 'star', since some of the early pennies were marked with a star. A 'pound sterling' was a pound weight of sterlings.

storey is of the same origin as 'story', and comes from the Latin word *historia* 'story, history'. *Historia* also meant 'picture' in England in the Middle Ages and it is likely that the meaning of 'storey' came about because of rows of painted windows on houses.

strand may be derived either from the Old French word *estran* 'rope', or Germanic *strang* 'rope, string'. Strand also has the meaning of 'land by the sea or water'.

street is from the Anglo-Saxon *straet*, and in turn from the Latin *strata* 'something thrown or laid down'. Languages related to English also have a similar word. In Dutch it is *straat*, and in German *strasse*.

stupid is from the Latin word *stupidus*, taken from the verb *stupere* 'to be amazed'. At one time, the word meant 'stunned with surprise', but took on its present meaning during the 16th century. 'Stupendous' is a similar word, but used in the original sense.

sugar comes from the Arabic *sukkar*, related to the Persian word *shakar* and the Greek word *sakchar*.

superman was not invented by those who devised the comic strip. In fact, the word was first used in English in 1903 by George Bernard Shaw for his play *Man and Superman*. It was an attempt to translate the German word *übermensch* used by the German writer Nietzsche. *Über* means 'over' and *mensch* is 'human being'.

swank is a dialect word first used in the English Midlands, becoming widely known throughout the English-speaking world during this century. It might come from the German *swanken* 'to sway', or be connected to the word 'swagger'.

swastika comes from the Sanskrit *svastika*, from *svasti*, meaning 'well-being, fortune'. The symbol is also called the 'fylfot' or 'gammadion'. It later became associated with the Nazi party in Germany, although the symbol is not German.

swindle is formed from swindler, 'a cheat', and comes from the German *schwindler*. This word was brought to England by German-Jewish immigrants in the 18th century. It originally applied to someone who cadged or begged.

syrup reached English from the French word *sirop*, but it came originally from the Arabic *sharab*, from *shariba* 'to drink'. These Arabic words were also the source of our word 'sherbet'.

T

tabernacle and **tavern** both come from the Latin word *tabernaculum*, which meant a 'tent, booth or shed'. It was derived from another Latin word *taberna*, meaning a 'hut or booth'. Both words were adapted in French, and then taken into English.

tambourine is taken from the French *tambourin*, and earlier *tambour* and *tabour*. This referred to a small drum. This word is found in Arabic as *tambur* 'lute', and in Persian as *taburak* 'drum'.

tank As a name for the armoured fighting vehicle, this word is of British origin. It was originally used during World War I as a secret code-name for the new vehicle. When the armoured vehicle came into use, the code-name 'tank' was kept. Its original meaning for 'cistern' comes from an Indian word *tankh* 'a reservoir'.

tarantula is taken from the town of Taranto, in Italy, where the spider is found.

tea is a word originally found in Amoy Chinese as *t'e*. It was adopted by the Dutch as *thee*, and so passed into European languages pronounced more or less as in English. The Mandarin Chinese word for 'tea' is *ch'a*, and so the Russians and Portuguese say *chai* or *cha*.

tennis comes from the French *tenez*, from *tenir* 'to hold'. In early times, the server shouted *tenes* to attract his or her opponent's attention.

terracotta is Italian, and literally means 'cooked earth'. The English use of the word to describe brownish-red unglazed pottery dates from the 18th century.

thesaurus is from the Greek word *thesauros*, meaning 'treasury', and was used in the early 19th century especially to describe a treasury of knowledge, or a treasury of words.

thug is from an Indian word *thag*, meaning a professional robber or murderer. It passed into English after it was used by the British army in India, and during the 19th century came to describe any cut-throat or ruffian.

ticket comes from the French word *étiquet*, formerly *estiquet* 'etiquette'. The French word came from the Old French verb *estiquer* 'to stick', which is from the German *stechen* with the same meaning.

tinsel is from the French word *étincelle* 'spark', which in turn is derived from the Latin *stincilla*.

tram once meant the shaft of a barrow

TARANTULA

or cart, and later applied to a kind of sledge or truck pulled along. The word 'tram' came to be applied to the track (made of wood, iron or stone) along which the trucks were pulled. When passenger vehicles were run on such tracks, they were called tramcars and this was later shortened to 'trams'.

treacle comes from the French *triacle*, a kind of salve or ointment used as an antidote to animal bites. Later it meant any kind of remedy, often in the form of a syrup. The word comes from Greek *theriake*, from *therion* 'wild beast' or 'poisonous animal'.

trinket originally meant a shoemaker's knife, and also had the meaning of a 'toy-knife' made especially for ladies to wear as ornaments on chains. It originates from the Old French *trenquer* 'to cut'.

truant once had the meaning of 'beggar, or idle rogue', but in the 16th century it took on the meaning of a pupil absent from school. It is originally a Celtic word, and is also related to the Welsh word *truan* and Gaelic *truaghan* 'wretched'.

tsar (or **czar**) is a Russian word derived from the Latin *Caesar*. It also appears in German as *kaiser*.

turban comes to English from Portuguese *turbante*. Its origin is in the Persian word *dulband*, with the 'd' altered to a 't' and the 'l' changed to an 'r'. The English word 'tulip' also comes from the same Persian word. The Turks called the flower *tuliband*, because the shape of a turban looked like the tulip.

typhoon seems to have had several separate origins which led to one word. One was the Chinese *tai fung* 'big wind'. The other was the Arabic *tufan* 'hurricane'. Greek also had *typhon* 'whirlwind'. Originally, the words cannot have been connected, so their similar meanings are a remarkable coincidence.

umbrella is from the early Italian word *ombrella*, which meant 'little shade', since the umbrella was originally used as a sunshade. It comes from the Latin word *umbra*, meaning 'shade'.

union, **unique**, **unit** and **unite** are all from the same source, the Latin *unus* 'one'. 'Unique' is derived from Latin *unicus* 'one and only', and 'unite' from the verb *unire* 'to join together'.

urchin once meant simply 'hedgehog'. In earlier times it was also used as a slang word for 'goblin' or 'small boy or brat'. It comes from the Old French *heriçon*, from Latin *ericius* 'hedgehog'.

vaccinate comes from Latin *vacca* 'a cow'. This is because Edward Jenner invented vaccination in 1798, after he noticed that people who had suffered from cowpox were unlikely to catch smallpox. The milder disease gave the sufferer immunity against the more dangerous one; vaccination worked in the same way.

vandal The Vandals were a German tribe that invaded Western Europe in the fourth and fifth centuries AD destroying many beautiful cities and objects. After its use in the 18th century by the French revolutionary, Henri Grégoire, destructive people became known as 'vandals'.

vermin has its origins in the Latin *verminum*, from *vermis* 'worm'. Originally it meant 'worms', but later came to be used of any unwanted animals.

vicinity comes from the Latin word *vicinitas*, in turn taken from *vicinus* 'neighbour' and *vicus* 'village'. The English suffix 'wick' in place-names comes from the same source.

Viking comes from the same source as 'vicinity', since the word is based on *vik* or *wic*, meaning a camp or village. The Vikings would make temporary camps whenever they made raids in other countries.

vitamin is an invented word, first used by the Polish-born American biochemist, Casimir Funk, in 1913. It is taken from Latin *vita* 'life', and the chemical *amine* (from ammonia).

volt is taken from the name of the Italian physicist and chemist, Alessandro Volta, and first came into use in 1827.

wafer originally meant a small flat cake with a honeycomb design. It is connected with the German word *wabe* 'honeycomb', but is also related to the English word 'weave'. From the same source comes the American word *waffle*.

water is a word which is found in many European languages with different spellings and varying pronunciation. In Dutch it is *water*, German has *wasser*, and in Russian it takes the form *voda*.

web once meant 'woven fabric' and can still be used in that sense. In the 13th century it was also used to mean 'cobweb' or 'tissue'.

Welsh is from the Old English word *waelisc*, meaning 'foreign'. It originates in the name of a Celtic tribe, known in Latin as the *Volcae*. It is the second part of the name 'Cornwall', and is found too in the name of the French-speaking Belgians, the 'Walloons'.

wigwam is taken from a North American Indian word. This word varies from tribe to tribe, as *wikiwam*, *weekuwom* or *wiquoam*, and means 'their house'.

window comes from the Early English word *windoge*, from the Old Norse word *vindauga* meaning 'wind-eye'. An early name in Anglo-Saxon times was *eagdura* 'eye-door'.

wistaria This plant was named in honour of the American anatomist Caspar Wistar (1761–1818).

worm has not always meant 'earthworm'. It was originally used to describe dragons and serpents. It comes from a Germanic root, but is related to Greek *rhomos* 'woodworm' and Latin *vermis* 'worm'.

wrong originally meant 'crooked, twisted or bent'. In Anglo-Saxon, the word was *wrang* meaning 'injustice'. It took on the meaning of 'incorrect' in about the 13th century.

yoga is a Hindi word meaning 'union with the Supreme Spirit', and is taken from a similar word in Sanskrit, meaning 'union'. A 'yogi' is one who practises meditation.

xylophone takes its name from two Greek words, *xylo* 'wood' and *phonos* 'sound'. This is because the instrument is made of flat wooden bars.

zany is from the Italian *zanni*, which is simply a dialect form of the name 'John' – *Giovanni*. A zany was originally a kind of comic performer; a sort of clown's assistant. Later it was used to mean a simpleton or idiot.

zest originally had the meaning of orange or lemon peel used as a flavouring and it still retains that meaning. Its other meaning of 'relish' or 'gusto' came into use during the 18th century. The word comes from the French *zeste*.

Yiddish is taken from the German word *jüdisch*, which means 'Jewish'. In German, the word is pronounced very much as it is spelled in English.